I Am Priceless

ANGELA RUTLEDGE

I Am Priceless

ISBN 979-8-9896701-0-9

CONTENTS

I'm Damaged

"You don't know where I came from! You have no idea what I've done!" Sound familiar? Do you think you are the only one with a past? Do you feel you are the only one walking around trying to hide all the pain in your life? I hate to tell you you aren't that special, but you're not! The affluent adolescents, the ones living below poverty, and all those in-between, endure some of the same challenges as you.

The lies you tell yourself make you believe you are unlovable, unacceptable, and unwanted. Maybe you grew up in a family that fought all the time and you never truly understood what love looked like. It may

have led you to decide to make mature
decisions before you were really ready to
handle all that came with those decisions.
After all, sexting as well as sex is happening
in middle schools nowadays. If everybody is
doing it, why can't you?

Wait...the boy or girl you sent pictures to
decided to share them? WTH?!?! Well,
that sucks. Do you know someone who has
experienced that very thing? Do you know
someone who has, or have you, experienced
unwanted sexual contact? It was not your
fault. If the person doing the act told you it
was your fault, he or she is a liar. Possibly
nobody will believe you if you tell, but it WAS
NOT your fault.

Others handle life by choosing to cut
themselves as a soothing mechanism or
possibly starving themselves as the one
thing they can control. If you just got done

cutting or purging, you are still beautiful. You were created at the right time with a unique purpose. I know it is hard to keep going some days. I know how hard it is to contain the cries for help when everyone around you only sees your smile. Please keep going.

Did you experience what you thought would be a private moment, yet everyone somehow found out about it? Have you been the target of gossip or cyber bullying? Some people are going to talk about you no matter what you do. I promise. While they may be searching for the negative, someone else loves you for your positive attributes.

I really do not like the old adage "One man's trash is another man's treasure," but I can understand life is about perspective. You are NOT trash. You are TREASURE!!! You are still here today reading these words.

Yesterday is over. Focus on today. Tomorrow will present its own set of circumstances.

Your past has certainly influenced your thoughts, your health, your grades and maybe your self-esteem. Even so, your "damage" does not define or cheapen you. You are not a clearance shelf item just because life happened to you, or you made some immature decisions. When you are trying so hard to fit the societal messages of who you should be, remember, Hollywood often leaves the really real stuff out. TikTok, IG, Snapchat, and YouTube are platforms to showcase your best version of yourself. It's like the waxed apples in the store attempting to make you believe they were picked yesterday from someone's orchard. In reality, they are weeks old trying to hide any damage which would lead you to believe you picked a bad one.

I know you can detail the destructiveness of life with ease, as well as any perceived flaws. It is much easier to point out our flaws instead of cheering for ourselves.

QUESTIONS

How have the trying times of life taught you new skills? Maybe you have learned how to pack or get dressed in a matter of minutes. Maybe you can differentiate between what you thought was necessary and now know to be necessary.

What are some things you love about you?

What characteristics make you unique?

What do others complement you on?

I AM PRICELESS

NOTES

_____

_____

_____

_____

_____

_____

_____

_____

_____

_____

I AM PRICELESS

CHAPTER 02

I'm Stuck

Have you ever been sitting in class taking a test and have no idea what you're doing? Did you feel stuck? Like, "Well, the teacher isn't going to help me. I can't ask Siri or Alexa or search Quizlet. I have to come up with something." Maybe you felt stuck in a class with the boy or girl you used to date. What about stuck in an educational track your parents made you pick? Possibly you feel stuck in your state and hometown. All of these can lead to frustration. Am I right? I felt all of those as well as some deeper forms of being stuck as a young woman coming into my own. How do you overcome?

Unfortunately, you may not get to choose where you go to school or what type of car you get to drive, if any. You most definitely did not get a say in who your family would be. Nonetheless, you are right where you should be. I will talk you through some easy steps to get unstuck. First and foremost, you must acknowledge if you are spinning your wheels while going nowhere fast or maybe you are a numb passenger watching life pass you by. Instead of constant states, these may be places you have visited.

Next, look back at how you got to where you are today. Take a moment to reflect on what landed you here. Was it your parents lack of parenting skills? Was it your friends deciding to become cliquish and leaving you out? Did you outgrow your friends? What about how hormones truly do mess with everything from your mood to your face to your weight to your taste in food and friends? Could it have been your own choices and the consequences of those choices?

Are you living the fast life you thought would bring you happiness or wondering when you'll get noticed or possibly hoping you can sail through life off the radar entirely? Has fear paralyzed you? Are you afraid of doing the wrong thing. Is it terrifying to consider leaving familiarity behind?

Just because you made mistakes does not mean you are not allowed to decide to be different. If you are beating yourself up over what you did or didn't do right, you are letting life pass you by. Every single moment of every single day is time you will never get back. Decide right now who you think you want to be going forward. Write it down on your mirror. Post it on your story. Add it to your notes. So, you can go back and see where you want to go. Getting unstuck starts with acknowledging where you are, before worrying so much about where you think you'll end up. The first step is the hardest, but you got this!

QUESTIONS

In what areas are you stuck?

What would it look like to be unstuck?

Do you feel at peace with who and where you are now?

If not, what would that type of peace look like and how would it make you feel?

NOTES

I AM PRICELESS

CHAPTER 03

I Don't Know How

I would have to say the best thing about living today is you can find out how to do just about anything, from cooking to painting to fixing a car or computer, almost instantaneously! But, the most important thing you can do is search for information on how to be better. It may come from your parents, whom you may not want to listen to currently. Even so, try to pick out the nuggets of good information they do offer. Additionally, teachers, coaches, pastors, and tutors are great resources. They will each provide a unique perspective on the advice they give, yet listen with open ears.

Once you've searched for information in the digital world and gather advice from some folks who have had time to make mistakes, you will have a basis of how to change your mindset. Your mind keeps you from going forward a good deal of the time. The lies and negative self-talk trap you in the sinking sand of "not good enough." Forget that mess. Tie a rope of truth around yourself and allow the truth to set you free.

I would say one of the hardest things to do is change your friends. Yet, if you are surrounded with people who constantly remind you of why you'll never succeed, you need a new friend group. I'd rather soar as an eagle alone than be hunted by wolves surrounded with my sheeple! Associates are great. True friends are way better! You cannot get unstuck alone. It will take knowledge and assistance. Be willing to do the hard work.

QUESTIONS

Where have you tried to garner information before?

How will your search for knowledge change now?

Take an inventory of the life givers in your circle. Who are some people you can go to for help?

What's stopping you from asking?

If you have "none," seek out one person and be willing to be vulnerable with him or her.

Are there any books you've read, or want to read, to help encourage you on your journey?

I AM PRICELESS

_____

_____

_____

_____

_____

_____

_____

_____

_____

_____

I AM PRICELESS

CHAPTER 04

I Have to Listen

Yes! You are going to have to listen. Have you ever tried to make a new recipe without seeking help? How did it turn out? I'm thinking of the breakfast in bed you made for your parents when you were little. My guess is it consisted of cereal, maybe oatmeal, some toast and juice. Those are all relatively easy to do if you've watched someone else prepare it before. What about Eggs Benedict with smoked salmon and freshly squeezed orange juice? Maybe you are one of the few who always enjoyed cooking, but even still at some point you had to follow some sort of recipe to come up with something similar to your intended dish.

Life is much the same. What's the point of taking a personal assessment, doing research on how to change and then choosing to ignore it? Do you want to stay stuck? Is getting unstuck harder than you anticipated? It reminds me of when my mom thought I should join the track team. I thought it would be easy and fun to run the sprints. In my mind, I thought my practice would consist of only sprints. After all, I was not there to be a distance runner. Yet, the coach made all of us run what seemed like 10 miles!!! I thought that was cruel and unusual punishment. Now, I understand it was to build up endurance, but then I thought he was just crazy.

The thought of change may seem hard. It may even be scary to modify your old habits and thought patterns. Nonetheless, change is essential to your growth. I hope you are excited to try something different and you're willing to do what it takes to truly adopt new patterns. The new information is like braces meant to help straighten your thoughts. Likewise, the retainer would be like friends and mentors who hold you accountable to changing.

QUESTIONS

How have you been able to incorporate what you have learned thus far?

What has been the most challenging part?

Could it have been asking for help in the first place?

Does listening to others come easy for you or not so much? Why/why not?

I AM PRICELESS

NOTES

I AM PRICELESS

CHAPTER 05

I Have a Cheering Squad

YES!!! More people than not want you to succeed, including me! I want you to see yourself as the beautiful creation you are: loved and valued! Regardless of what your current situation looks like or where you live or what your background is. I want you to figure out what you were designed to do because only you can do it the way you would! I think I'm pretty good at hugs, but I know another who gives WAY better hugs than me. Although you may think hugs are meaningless or not such a big deal, a hug can entirely change the trajectory of someone's day or week or life.

Those people who poured their wealth of knowledge into you are your cheering squad. They want you to keep on learning and perfecting your craft(s). Believe it or not, even the naysayers are a part of your cheering squad. They are watching you continue to soar, possibly in disbelief. They may be jealous, impressed, or downright confused as to how you went from stuck to soaring. Your squad may be only one other person currently. Perhaps you already had a cheering squad before starting this journey. Your squad will evolve and grow as you embark on the journey to adulthood.

Accountability is essential to lasting change. Personal accountability is key to ensuring you recognize when you are not where you need to be mentally, physically or emotionally. I've heard breaking an old habit takes 21 days. Yet, I would say it takes a *lifetime*. If you fall back into old habits or even just stop...that is okay.

Start with today and keep it moving. Thankfully, you can always reach out to your squad when you feel like you're lost or slipping back into old ways.

QUESTIONS

One of the best feelings is having others clap and chant your name as you cross the finish line—of a race, degree, project, or etc. How does it feel knowing others want you to succeed?

What can you do to motivate yourself?

Do you have a song you listen to, a picture to ponder on, or maybe a verse or encouraging word you've heard?

Have you written down goals or task lists for yourself to accomplish?

How do you feel when you can check them off because they are accomplished?

I AM PRICELESS

NOTES

I AM PRICELESS

CHAPTER 06

I Will Forgive, Trust & Love

Why on earth would I forgive, trust and love? Who needs my forgiveness, trust or love? Great questions! Decide today to forgive anyone who has hurt you in the past as well as forgiving yourself for making mistakes. This really is much harder than the lip service we sometimes give. You cannot forgive a person for really hurting you in a day or so. Choosing not to talk about whatever happened does not mean you have forgiven either. Acknowledge your hurts and your feelings associated with the hurts. Understand the person who used to be your best friend or the troll on your page may never ask for forgiveness. Still, the forgiveness is so you can move on with your life.

Trust is hard to give and easy to lose. Plenty of people have broken my trust. Unfortunately, their mistake made it harder for me to trust others again afterwards. It is not impossible though. You do not have to be naïve, trusting everyone blindly. Use what you have learned to help you decipher the level of trust you can give. Stages of trust start with sharing basic information about yourself and grow to trusting wholeheartedly.

Have you seen those HWLF bracelets? I once saw a young lady wearing one and asked what it meant. "He Would Love First," was her answer. It's a complement or answer to the "What Would Jesus Do" WWJD bracelets. I thought for a minute about how different the world would be if we all loved each other like ourselves. Then, I thought…

maybe we do. If we have a broken sense of self due the past trauma and mistakes, we are not really loving in the way I think love was intended.

Do you "love" messages your friends send? "Love" posts on social media? That's not the kind of love I am talking about. I mean, you have to love others as though they will not hurt you like those who have let you down in the past. Inevitably, someone else will hurt you. Forgive them because you will also hurt someone else on this journey called life. We are not perfect.

QUESTIONS

List any people you may need to forgive, including yourself. What actions do you need to forgive?

Has it been challenging for you to trust others? If so, why?

How can you work on developing and maintaining healthy trust with boundaries?

What does love look like coming from you? From others?

I AM PRICELESS

_____

_____

_____

_____

_____

_____

_____

_____

_____

_____

I AM PRICELESS

CHAPTER 07

I AM PRICELESS

You are PRICELESS! Yep. You! You are the only you! You are as rare as the latest diamond unearthed. You are as valuable as all the gold in the world. You are unique. Once you realize your worth, you can stop letting comparison rob you of your joy and happiness. Comparison lies, making you believe you cannot be as successful as _____; you are not as talented as _____; you will never be loved, accepted, or _____. WRONG! You can be confident in who you are and your purpose here. Nothing can stop you, except you!

Determine what is holding you back from launching into who you want to be—trauma, past, or ignorance. Acknowledge the fears and mistakes. Ask for help! Apply what you've learned along the way to see how you add value to others. Slowing down may happen, but quitting is NOT an option! Trust the process. Forgive and love yourself. Get up and shine! Your light will not diminish because someone around you is also shining. Go become your best self.

AFFIRMATIONS

Write affirmations for yourself!

List out your favorite things about yourself.

If you have moments or even days when you do not feel priceless, reflect on your progress and let it propel you forward!

Remember this is a marathon with the prize being a healthy, realistic view of yourself!

I AM PRICELESS

_____

_____

_____

_____

_____

_____

_____

_____

_____

NOTES

I AM PRICELESS

_____

_____

_____

_____

_____

_____

_____

_____

_____

_____

Crisis
National Child Abuse Hotline
1-800-422-4453
www.childhelphotline.org

National Domestic Violence Hotline
1-800-799-7233,
SMS: Text START to 88788
www.thehotline.org

National Sexual Assault Hotline
1-800-656-4673 www.rainn.org

National Suicide and Crisis Lifeline
Call/Text 988

StopBullying.gov
www.stopbullying.gov

Substance Abuse and Mental Health
Services Administration (SAMHSA)
1-800-662-4537, https://findtreatment.gov/

Mentoring

Big Brothers Big Sisters of America
www.bbbs.org

Boys and Girls Clubs of America
www.bgca.org

MENTOR
www.mentoring.org

YMCA
www.ymca.org

www.ingramcontent.com/pod-product-compliance
Lightning Source LLC
Chambersburg PA
CBHW060956120626
46557CB00003B/1186